34880000 8 23174

BOOK CHARGING CARD

Accession No. _____ Call No. 974.3 FOR

Author Foran, Jill

Title Vermont

Date | Date

974.3
FOR

Foran, Jill
Vermont

34880000823174

VERMONT

Jill Foran

Published by Weigl Publishers Inc.
123 South Broad Street, Box 227
Mankato, MN   56002
USA
Web site: http://www.weigl.com

Library of Congress Cataloging-in-Publication Data available upon
request from the publisher. Fax: (507) 388-2746 for the attention of the
Publishing Records Department.

ISBN 1-930954-54-9

Printed in the United States of America
1 2 3 4 5 6 7 8 9 10   05 04 03 02 01

Editor
Jennifer Nault
Copy Editor
Jared Keen
Designer
Warren Clark
Terry Paulhus
Photo Researchers
Joe Nelson
Tina Schwartzenberger

Photograph Credits
Every reasonable effort has been made to trace ownership and to obtain
permission to reprint copyright material. The publishers would be
pleased to have any errors or omissions brought to their attention so
that they may be corrected in subsequent printings.

Cover: man tapping maple tree, Green Mountains, (Kindra Clineff Photography);
Steve Allen: pages 20T, 26B; **Archives Nationales du Quebec:** page 17T; **Kindra
Clineff Photography:** pages 4T, 6B, 8T, 9BL, 9BR, 14T, 15BL, 15BR, 17B, 18B, 20BR;
Corbis Corporation: page 22B; **Bettman/Corbis:** pages 18T, 25B; **Corel Corporation:**
pages 3M, 11T, 11B, 19B, 29L; **EyeWire Corporation:** pages 13BR, 14B, 24BR, 27T;
National Archives of Canada: pages 16BL (C-61336), 28T (PA-138682); **New
Hampshire Historical Society:** page 16T; **PhotoDisc Corporation:** pages 13BL, 26T,
29R; **Photofest:** page 24T; **PhotoSpin Corporation:** pages 3B, 22T, 28B; **Courtesy of
the Shelburne Museum:** pages 12T, 12B, 23T; **Utah Historical Society:** page 23B;
Vermont Department of Tourism and Marketing: pages 4B, 5, 6T, 7T, 7B, 8B, 9T, 13T,
15T, 20BL, 21T, 21B, 24BL, 25T; **J. Weaver/Vermont Department of Tourism and
Marketing:** pages 10B, 19T; **Vermont Wildflower Farm/Vermont Department of
Tourism and Marketing:** pages 3T, 10T; **Heather Cook/Courtesy of the Vermont
Expos:** page 27B; **Marilyn "Angel" Wynn:** page 16BR.

CONTENTS

Vermont's many mountains are covered with evergreens such as spruce, hemlock, and fir.

INTRODUCTION

"Good things come in small packages." That saying aptly describes the state of Vermont. In addition to being one of the smallest states in the nation, Vermont also has one of the lowest populations. This makes it one of the only rural states in the country. Despite its small size, a great deal of history, culture, and natural beauty is packed into Vermont. Sprawling across the northeastern region are the lovely Green Mountains. Its culture is equally fascinating, with large German and French-Canadian communities. Vermont has an exciting past. In fact, after the original thirteen colonies, Vermont was the first to join the Union. Vermonters have strong ties to their history, and in many ways, the state's history helped shape the nation. Even today, visitors to Vermont may feel as though they have stepped back in time. It is a place where farm fields lie alongside small towns and villages.

QUICK FACTS

The capital of Vermont is Montpelier. With a population of less than 10,000 residents, Montpelier is the smallest state capital in the nation.

Five villages in Vermont are too small to have local governments—Averill, Ferdinand, Glastenbury, Lewis, and Somerset. The largest of the five is Ferdinand, with a population of twenty-eight people.

Vermont covers an area of about 9,600 square miles. It ranks forty-third in size among all the states.

Two U.S. presidents were from Vermont. Chester A. Arthur was the twenty-first president, and Calvin Coolidge was the thirtieth.

Montpelier is located in central Vermont, where the Winooski and North Branch Rivers meet.

Getting There

Vermont is part of the New England region, an area located in the northeast corner of the country. Of all the New England states, Vermont is the only one that does not have an Atlantic Ocean coastline. Despite Vermont's inland location, water borders more than half of the state. The Connecticut River forms the state's entire eastern border, and Lake Champlain and the Poultney River flow along part of its western border. Vermont's neighbors are New York State to the west, New Hampshire to the east, Massachusetts to the south, and the Canadian province of Quebec to the north.

There are many ways to get to Vermont. Interstate highways provide easy access to most of the state's cities and towns. For visitors who prefer air travel, there are seventeen public airports. The largest and busiest airport in Vermont is the Burlington International Airport. Lake Champlain is also a popular transportation route.

QUICK FACTS

Lake Champlain ranks as the sixth-largest body of fresh water in the United States.

The state song is "These Green Mountains," written by Diane B. Martin and Rita Buglass Gluck.

Vermont has 14,251 miles of highways and 540 miles of railroad track.

Trains are another way to get to the state. The Vermonter provides daily rail service from Washington, D.C. to nine stops within Vermont.

Ferries bring passengers from various points in New York to Burlington, Grand Isle, Charlotte, or Larabees Point.

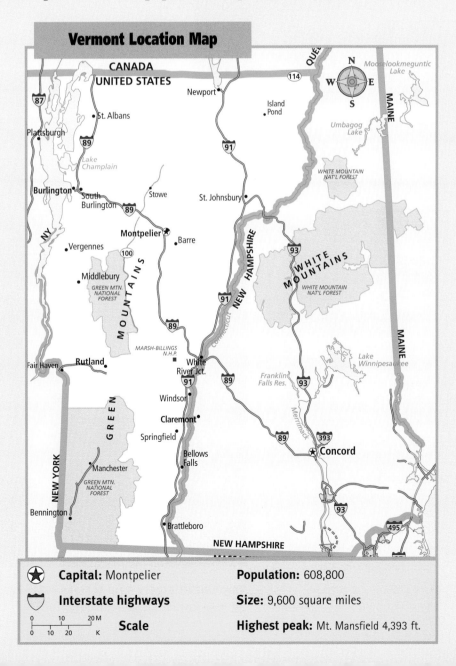

Vermont Location Map

Capital: Montpelier   **Population:** 608,800

Interstate highways   **Size:** 9,600 square miles

Scale   **Highest peak:** Mt. Mansfield 4,393 ft.

Vermont's historic covered bridges are popular tourist attractions.

Vermont's history and landscape have connections to the state's name. The name "Vermont" is derived from the French words "*vert mont*," which mean "green mountain." Vermont is known for its Green Mountains—they are the backbone of the state. Every year, thousands of tourists come to Vermont to enjoy the many recreational activities that the Green Mountains have to offer. The ridges of these beautiful peaks can be seen from almost every part of the state. Their prominence has earned Vermont its nickname—"The Green Mountain State."

The name "Green Mountain" also refers to the state's early history. When the American Revolution began in 1775, Vermont's Green Mountain Boys helped to fight against British rule. Under the command of Vermonter Ethan Allen, the Green Mountain Boys captured Fort Ticonderoga and Crown Point from the British. They fought against British rule, but the Green Mountain Boys also fought against New York's claim to their land. They raided the New York settlements, chasing many New Yorkers out of the area.

QUICK FACTS

Vermont grew tired of land disputes and declared their region an independent republic in 1777. They remained a successful independent republic for fourteen years.

On March 4, 1791, after all the land disputes had been settled, Vermont became the fourteenth state to join the Union.

There are 114 covered bridges in Vermont. The bridges were built with roofs and walls so that the wooden **trusses** would be protected from decay.

Burlington is the largest city in Vermont.

Vermont is largely a rural state—this makes for interesting traffic on some of its unpaved roads.

Vermont's state tree is the sugar maple. The sap of this tree supports the maple syrup industry.

QUICK FACTS

Among Vermont's major rivers are the Connecticut, Missisquoi, Lamoille, Winooski, White, Otter Creek, West, and Battenkill.

Vermont's state mineral is talc, and its state gem is the grossular garnet.

Environmental conservation is in full force at Vermont's ski areas. From recycling to energy conservation, many work to preserve the environment and help to maintain the state's natural beauty.

Vermont has six state forests, the largest of which is Mount Mansfield State Forest.

Just about four out of five Vermonters live in small villages and towns. This makes Vermont one of the few rural states in the country. Many people in Vermont value the peace and quiet that rural life has to offer. Small towns tend to differ from big cities. For instance, town centers are usually quieter and less smoggy than city centers. Even Vermont's urban centers are small. Residents treasure the unspoiled land, and many make efforts to preserve their environment.

Vermont's environment is not only beautiful—it is also one of the state's most profitable features. Many visitors are drawn to Vermont by the state's impressive landscape. The greatest draws by far are the excellent ski areas and ski resorts—especially in the Green Mountains. Snowboarders and skiers can choose from more than 5,700 acres of hills in the state, which range from gentle slopes to extreme runs. A great number of skiers head to the town of Stowe, which receives about 250 inches of snowfall every year. As Stowe is the location of the highest mountain in the state, expert skiers from around the world come here to conquer the challenging "Big Four" runs.

The Stowe Gondola whisks passengers to the top of Mount Mansfield, where people can enjoy a view that encompasses New York, Massachusetts, and New Hampshire.

The land in Vermont is extremely fertile. The state receives, on average, 50 inches of rain every year.

QUICK FACTS

There are 223 mountains that are over 2,000 feet in height in Vermont. The tallest mountain in the state is Mount Mansfield, which stands 4,393 feet high.

The largest lake entirely within Vermont is Lake Bomoseen.

Vermont's mountains and valleys are usually blanketed in snow for at least five months every year. The state's winters are generally long and cold, and its summers are short and cool. Summer evening temperatures drop quickly, especially in the mountains.

The lowest recorded temperature in Vermont was a chilly –50° Fahrenheit, on December 30, 1933.

LAND AND CLIMATE

Vermont is made up of six main land regions. The White Mountain region is found in the northeastern corner of the state. The mountains of this region are mostly granite. The Western New England Upland region covers most of eastern Vermont. This zone consists of rolling uplands that give way to lowlands. The Green Mountains region runs through central Vermont, stretching from the state's northern border to its southern border. These mountains are heavily forested. The Vermont Valley region is a narrow strip of land in the southwestern part of the state. The Taconic Mountain range is also found in the southwest. The highest mountain of this range is Mount Equinox, measuring 3,816 feet. The name *Taconic* is thought to have come from an Algonquian word referring to a tree, a wood, or a forest. Lastly, the sixth land region is the Champlain Valley, which borders Lake Champlain. The lowland valley is home to some of the state's most fertile farmland.

Mount Mansfield, Vermont's highest peak, is estimated to be about 380 million years old.

Fruit and vegetable markets are common sights in Vermont.

NATURAL RESOURCES

Although Vermont is small, its borders harbor a wealth of natural resources. These include dense forests and valuable mineral and rock deposits. The state's principle mining location is the Green Mountains region. Granite, slate, and marble are found in this area. Granite is the state's leading mined product. In fact, the largest granite **quarries** in the United States—and some of the world's largest—are located around Barre.

With about 80 percent of the state covered by forests, Vermont's trees are an important natural resource. Lumber and plywood are the leading wood products. Vermont is also the largest producer of maple syrup in the United States. Syrup producers begin to collect sap from maple trees in early spring—known as "the sugaring season"—when sap begins to flow. Syrup producers drive a metal spout into one or more holes in each tree. A bucket is hung from each spout to collect sap. Buckets are emptied into a large barrel, which is taken to a building called a sugarhouse. In the sugarhouse, the sap is boiled until pure maple syrup remains. The color and flavor also develop during this process.

QUICK FACTS

The first marble quarry in the United States was opened in Vermont, at East Dorset. Isaac Underhill established the quarry in 1785.

Most of Vermont is covered by thin, stony soils that are difficult to cultivate. However, grass grows well in these soils, so much of the land is used as pasture for livestock. More fertile soil is found in the Champlain Valley.

Another way to obtain maple syrup is with the more modern pipeline system. The sap runs through tubes that are connected to the spouts and drained into a pipeline that connects to the sugarhouse. This method requires less time and labor.

PLANTS AND ANIMALS

It is difficult to believe that only 150 years ago, Vermont had almost no forests. Most of the forests had been cleared for agriculture. Since the 1850s, Vermonters have worked hard to regain and maintain their woodlands. Today, trees dominate the Vermont landscape. Most of the trees are **deciduous** and include species, such as maple, elm, birch, oak, and cherry. Each fall, the leaves on these trees change color, displaying shades of vivid red, purple, orange, and gold. **Conifers**, which are commonly found in Vermont's mountain areas, include white pines, hemlocks, and cedars.

Other types of plant life also flourish in Vermont. Red clover, the state flower, is used as animal feed and is also beneficial to farmland. Clover adds valuable **nitrogen** to the soil and increases the availability of other nutrients for certain crops. The most common wildflowers that decorate the state are buttercups, goldenrods, daisies, violets, and lilacs.

The white, oxeye daisy is the most common wild daisy in North America.

QUICK FACTS

Green Mountain National Forest covers 353,757 acres of scenic woodlands and mountain peaks.

Autumn in Vermont is known as the "foliage season," when leaves on the trees change color. It usually begins in mid-September and continues into October.

The state is a leader in environmental awareness. In 1970, it passed the Environmental Control Law. This law allows the state to limit major development that could be harmful to the environment.

More than 80 percent of Vermont's forestland is privately owned.

Chlorophyll production decreases during autumn, causing the leaves to change color. They turn brown when pigment production has ended.

Most otters weigh between 10 and 30 pounds and are between 3 and 4 feet long, including their tail.

QUICK FACTS

In all, about fifty-eight species of mammals inhabit the Green Mountain State.

Bird-watchers are kept very busy in Vermont—more than 240 species of birds are found in the state.

The state bird is the hermit thrush. The honeybee is Vermont's official insect.

Vermont has many raccoons. Raccoons live on the ground and in trees. They usually hunt for food at night and stay in their dens during the day.

Vermont's forests are home to a variety of animals, including skunks, raccoons, minks, rabbits, squirrels, and woodchucks. White-tailed deer are also a common sight throughout many of the state's wooded areas. Larger animals, such as bears, moose, and bobcats, live in the higher mountain regions of Vermont.

Various waterfowl can be found bobbing on Vermont's lakes. Ducks, loons, and Canada geese are just a few of the birds that visit the area. The quiet waters and wetlands of the Missisquoi National Wildlife Refuge attract large flocks of **migratory** birds. This refuge is located on the eastern shore of Lake Champlain and provides 6,338 acres of protected animal habitat. Beavers, bullfrogs, snapping turtles, and otters also live in Vermont's wetland areas. Otters belong to the weasel family. These playful animals are expert swimmers and divers, and they can remain underwater for three or four minutes. They live close to water because they move awkwardly on land.

TOURISM

Every year, more than 4.6 million people visit the Green Mountain State. Vermont's beautiful scenery and its many recreational opportunities make it a popular year-round vacation spot. In the fall, tourists travel to the state to see the spectacular, changing colors of the trees. During the winter months, visitors arrive in Vermont to enjoy its first-rate ski facilities. Springtime brings the maple syrup harvest, when people travel to the state to watch this sweet, sticky liquid being made. In the summer, tourists take pleasure in outdoor activities, such as hiking, fishing, and camping.

Vermont is a great place for history buffs. A variety of historical attractions are found throughout the state. One of Vermont's most popular attractions is the Shelburne Museum, in Burlington. This museum consists of more than thirty historic buildings, including an 1890 railroad station, a lighthouse, and a stagecoach inn. A 200-foot steamship is also on the grounds. Another interesting historical attraction is the Vermont Historical Society Museum, in Montpelier, which traces the history of the state since the time of its earliest settlers, who arrived in the 1600s.

The steamboat *Ticonderoga* is one of the last remaining paddle-wheel passenger steamers in the United States.

QUICK FACTS

Visitors can explore the history of Lake Champlain at the Lake Champlain Maritime Museum. A boathouse, which is part of the museum, displays boats made by local residents.

The Rock of Ages Granite Quarry in Graniteville is considered to be one of the world's largest quarries. Its visitor's center presents informative exhibits, including a film about quarrying.

Windsor's Old Constitution House, which is open to visitors, is the site of the formation and adoption of the state's first constitution.

The General Store at the Shelburne Museum was built in 1840 and served as the village post office for many years to follow.

Southeast of Barre, is the Rock of Ages Granite Quarry. Sheer cliffs drop 475 feet to the quarry floor.

INDUSTRY

Manufacturing is the most important economic activity in Vermont, supporting a variety of industries. The service industry, however, employs the most people—about two-thirds of Vermont's workers. In manufacturing, the state produces more than $2 billion worth of goods each year. The production of electrical equipment, such as **semiconductors**, is Vermont's leading manufacturing activity. IBM, one of the world's largest electronics companies, has a large plant in Burlington. IBM has been in Vermont since 1957, and today, the company has approximately 8,000 full-time employees in the state. Other kinds of manufacturing include jet aircraft engines, which are made in the Rutland area, and large-scale machinery, which is produced in the Springfield and Windsor regions.

QUICK FACTS

Fabricated-metal products rank third among the state's top manufactured items. Machine tools and precision metal parts are the leading types of fabricated metal products.

There are forty-one newspapers published in Vermont, nine of which are dailies.

It is not difficult to find reading material in Vermont. Following electrical equipment, publishing is a major manufacturing industry in the state. Books, business forms, and newspapers are the leading products.

Semiconductor chips are a common component in most electronic systems, such as computers and video game consoles.

Fruit, vegetable, and other kinds of crops bring in nearly $23 million annually to Vermont's economy.

GOODS AND SERVICES

A pancake would not be complete if it were not for two of Vermont's key food products—butter and maple syrup. With farms occupying about 25 percent of the land, agriculture is a vital industry in Vermont. Dairy farming is the most profitable agricultural activity. In fact, Vermont leads all the other New England states in milk production. In addition to milk and butter, other dairy products that are exported to different parts of the country include cheese and ice cream. With its many maple trees, Vermont also exports a great deal of maple syrup.

Transporting Vermont's goods within the state was not always simple. Moving goods east–west through the Green Mountains had been difficult, and sometimes, very dangerous. Thanks to many road improvements, especially in places where roads approach streams, the difficulty of moving goods within the state has diminished. The Vermont Agency of Transportation continues to support and develop transportation networks that keep people and goods on the move.

Vermont has about 14,000 miles of highways and roads.

More than 2.5 billion pounds of milk are produced in Vermont each year. The state produces more than 100 million pounds of cheese annually.

Tourism has been a major contributor to the development of Vermont's service industry. Thousands of tourists visit the state each year, resulting in the creation and expansion of excellent resorts, hotels, restaurants, retail shops, and recreation facilities. In fact, just the hotel industry employs approximately 11,000 people. Tourism has also been instrumental in the move to improve the state's roads and other transportation systems. The service industry is the fastest growing sector of the state's economy.

A good education is important to Vermonters. The state's first public school was established in 1761, and in 1777, it became **mandatory** that each town in Vermont have a public school. Today, there are 376 public elementary and secondary schools in Vermont and more than 40 private schools. The state is also home to twenty-five post-secondary institutions, the oldest of which is the University of Vermont, founded in Burlington in 1791. About 45,000 students attend the state's post-secondary schools, which employ more than 8,500 people.

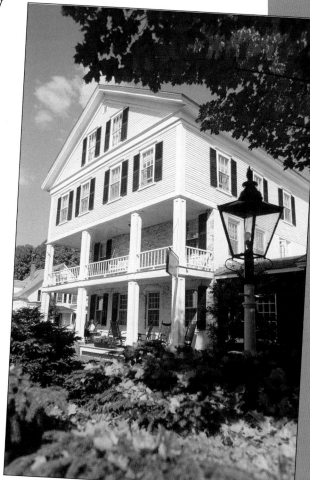

Tourism is Vermont's second-largest industry, providing more than $1.7 billion to the economy. While in Vermont, many tourists choose to stay at a quaint bed-and-breakfast.

Many Native Peoples in the Vermont area traveled via birchbark canoes.

FIRST NATIONS

The area now known as Vermont was first inhabited by a number of Native American groups from the Algonquian-speaking nation, including the Abenaki, the Mahican, and the Penacook. These peoples relied heavily on the region's abundant natural resources and supported themselves with fishing and hunting. They hunted using snares and traps, or bows and arrows. Each group consisted of small bands ruled by a chief, who advised the band members. The Abenaki, whose name means "people of the dawn," were the largest group to occupy the Vermont area. **Archeologists** have discovered evidence of Abenaki villages dating from the 1500s, or possibly prior, along the Connecticut River. Similar remains of Abenaki villages have also been found along Lake Champlain, near the mouth of the Winooski River.

The Iroquois inhabited the Vermont region, too. This powerful group, originally from what is now New York State, invaded areas along Lake Champlain. They managed to push most of the Algonquian groups out of the region long before any European explorers arrived. The Abenaki fought to defend their land from the Iroquois, and these two groups struggled for control of the area for many years.

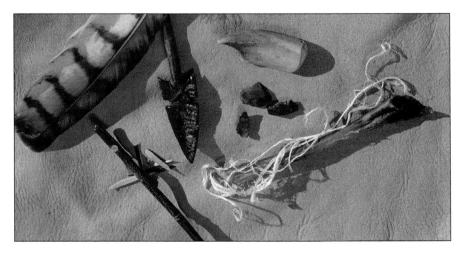

The discovery of Paleo-Indian tools has taught the modern world much about Vermont's early Native Peoples.

Samuel de Champlain was born in Brouage, France in 1567.

EXPLORERS AND MISSIONARIES

The first known European to set foot in the Green Mountains was a French explorer named Samuel de Champlain. He arrived in the Vermont area on July 4, 1609, via the lake that now bears his name. Champlain had left his encampment in Quebec so that he could join the Algonquin in a battle against their enemies, the Iroquois. With the help of their new French allies, the Abenaki were able to regain control over much of the territory that they had lost to the Iroquois, including their land in the Vermont region. However, Champlain claimed the entire region for France.

The British also claimed Vermont. For about 150 years after Champlain's visit, the French fought with the British for control of the Vermont region and the rest of North America. During this time, very few Europeans explored or settled in Vermont, but the Lake Champlain region became a major battleground.

QUICK FACTS

In 1666, the French built Fort Saint Anne on Isle La Motte.

British soldiers from the New York region built a fort at Chimney Point in 1690. This fort was used only as a temporary outpost during the land struggles between France and England, and like Fort Saint Anne, it was soon abandoned.

Native Peoples in the area took sides during the battles between France and England for control of North America. The Abenaki helped the French, while the Iroquois formed an alliance with the British.

Samuel de Champlain discovered Lake Champlain on July 4, 1609. To this day, the name "Lake Champlain" commemorates this early explorer.

EARLY SETTLERS

The first permanent European settlement in Vermont was established in 1724 near present-day Brattleboro. It was called Fort Drummer. During the following years, settlers from both New Hampshire and New York arrived in the Vermont area. From 1749 to 1763, the royal governor of New Hampshire made more than 130 grants of Vermont land, called the New Hampshire Grants. The question of who really owned the land was the source of many disputes when New York claimed the same land and granted it to other settlers.

In 1764, King George III, of England, ruled that New York had **jurisdiction** over Vermont. Settlers who held New Hampshire Grants were soon ordered to surrender their land or pay New York for it. In 1770, a number of the owners of New Hampshire Grants, most of whom were from Connecticut and Massachusetts, decided to defend their land. Under the leadership of Ethan Allen, they organized a military force called the Green Mountain Boys. Over the next five years, the Green Mountain Boys attacked many New York settlers and drove them out of Vermont.

In 1778, Ethan Allen petitioned the Continental Congress for Vermont's statehood. When Congress refused, he negotiated with the British to make Vermont a British province.

QUICK FACTS

Vermont was the last New England state to be settled.

England gained control of Vermont and much of the rest of North America after the French and Indian War, which lasted from 1754 to 1763.

Ethan Allen was born in Connecticut in 1738. He settled in the New Hampshire Grants, which is now Vermont. When he defended his land against settlers from New York, the governor of New York offered a large reward for Allen's arrest.

The Ethan Allen Homestead is a historic site and museum. It features a reconstructed version of Ethan Allen's Vermont home.

Vermont's trees were chopped down and used by early settlers as fuel to heat their homes.

Settlers in the region grew tired of the disputes over land rights. On January 15, 1777, representatives of the towns in the New Hampshire Grants declared their region an independent republic. They named it New Connecticut, and, six months later, changed the name to Vermont. The people of Vermont ran their independent republic for fourteen years. They coined their own money, established their own government, operated their own postal service, and **negotiated** with other states and countries. In 1790, New Hampshire agreed to give up its claim to Vermont. New York also gave up its claim in 1790, in exchange for $30,000. The following year, Vermont became the fourteenth state in the Union.

Vermont's population increased rapidly. In 1791, the area's population was about 85,000, but by 1810, more than 200,000 people were living in the state. A majority of the new Vermonters came from southern New England to farm. By 1830, the state's farmland no longer served as a lure for new settlers, but its growing manufacturing and mining industries were appealing. In the mid-1800s, many French-Canadian and Irish immigrants came to Vermont to work on its railroad or in one of its mills. In the late 1800s, many European immigrants came to work in the state's marble and granite quarries.

Vermont farmers sold half of their sheep as meat by 1860.

Among all the states, Vermont ranks forty-ninth in population. Only Wyoming has fewer people.

POPULATION

Vermont is considered the most rural state in the country. Almost 70 percent of the population live in villages or towns with fewer than 2,500 people. The rest of Vermonters live in the state's larger towns or cities, but even these urban centers are not highly populated. Burlington is by far Vermont's largest city, with a population of about 39,000 residents. The state's second largest city is Rutland, with about 17,500 people. Although these numbers are not large, the state's population has continued to grow steadily since the 1960s. Many new residents have come from neighboring states to work in Vermont's high-technology industries.

About 96 percent of the people living in Vermont were born in the United States. French Canadians, are the largest immigrant group. Most French Canadians in Vermont live in the Winooski area. People of Italian, Spanish, Welsh, and German descent also live in the state.

Vermont's rural population grew by 59 percent between 1960 and 1990, while the urban population grew by 21 percent.

Vermont's state flag depicts a pine tree, cow, sheaves of wheat, the Green Mountains, a stag's head, and the state motto.

QUICK FACTS

Vermont elects two senators and one representative to the United States Congress.

The state's 237 towns are run by local governments. Many government decisions are based on town meetings. Once a year, townspeople gather to elect town officials and to vote on matters, such as municipal budgets, school budgets, and town laws.

Vermont's Capitol is modeled after the nation's Capitol in Washington, D.C.

POLITICS AND GOVERNMENT

Vermont's original constitution was established in 1777. It was the first constitution in the United States to ban slavery and allow all men the right to vote, regardless of their income or property. Today, the state is governed under its third constitution, written in 1793. It is the shortest state constitution in the country.

Vermont's state legislature is called the General Assembly. Its structure is bicameral, which means that it consists of two houses. One house is the Senate, which is made up of thirty members. The other is the House of Representatives, which consists of 150 members. All serve two-year terms. The governor, who is also elected for a term of two years, is the head of the state's executive branch of government. Other elected members of the executive branch include the lieutenant governor, the secretary of state, and the treasurer.

The heritage of Vermont's Scottish population is celebrated with festivals across the state.

CULTURAL GROUPS

People of many different ethnic backgrounds have made their homes in the Green Mountain State. In 1724, the Dutch established a settlement in Pownal. In the 1880s, Vermont's booming granite industry attracted skilled craftspeople and quarry workers from all over Europe. The Barre region was the center of the granite industry. Italian and Scottish immigrants were among the largest groups to move to Barre. These groups worked to preserve many of the art forms and cultural traditions of their homelands. Some Scottish immigrants established a society called the Clan Gordon No. 12 of the Order of Scottish Clans. This society grew to become the largest Scottish society in the United States, with more than 500 members. In all, immigrants from about fifteen distinct ethnic groups moved to the Barre area to work in the granite industry. Many descendants of these groups continue to live in Vermont.

African Americans in Vermont make up 0.5 percent of the population.

At powwows, Native Peoples can preserve their cultural history.

QUICK FACTS

Some Abenaki still live in Vermont. They share their culture with visitors to the Shelburne Museum's annual Native-American **Powwow**. Representatives of other Native-American groups throughout the country also participate in this powwow, which features drumming, dancing, and storytelling.

Norwich University has been home to a prominent Russian school, where students study Russian culture and language.

People of east European descent honor their heritage at the Slavic Fair and Festival in Norfolk.

Vermont's thriving **textile** industry also appealed to immigrants in the 1800s. A significant number of French-Canadian immigrants came to work in the state's textile mills. Many French Canadians settled in Winooski, and soon, a portion of the community became known as French Village. Today, in Winooski, the French-speaking population is large enough that the local cable television system broadcasts French-language programs. Many of Vermont's French Canadians celebrate their distinct culture at Randolph's New World Festival.

Most of the people living in Vermont were born in the United States, but many are descendants of the state's early French, British, Scottish, and German settlers. Each year, Vermonters hold a variety of events to celebrate their various cultures. For example, the towns of Stowe, Bolton Valley, and West Dover celebrate German heritage with Oktoberfest. People of Scottish descent celebrate their heritage with the Quechee Scottish Festival. This festival features bagpiping competitions and Highland dancing. A stage showcases musical acts, such as fiddlers and **balladeers**. When attendees get hungry, they can sample some traditional Scottish food, including meat pies and **haggis**.

Early Mormon leader Brigham Young was born in Vermont.

ARTS AND ENTERTAINMENT

Maria von Trapp was active in the daily operations of the Trapp Family Lodge until her death in 1987.

Vermont's "hills are alive with the sound of music," thanks to the Trapp Family Singers. The Trapps, upon which the ever-popular film *The Sound of Music* is based, moved to Vermont in 1939. While giving musical performances across the country, the Trapps fell in love with Stowe, a tiny mountain town. They moved there because it reminded them of their homeland of Austria. Trapp mother, Maria, founded the Trapp Family Music Company in 1947. This eventually became the Trapp Family Lodge, which is still in operation.

From bluegrass to jazz, music is important to the Green Mountain State. Vermont is known for its many first-rate music schools. Brattleboro's Jazz Center offers jazz classes and workshops, and also features lively concert performances. In the summer, Marlboro College hosts the International Center for Advanced Musical Studies. Musicians from across the nation pack up their instruments and head to Vermont to study chamber music. Killington is also known for its summer musical training. Talented classical musicians from around the country travel to Vermont to teach and perform at the Killington Music Festival.

Traditionally, bluegrass has been a popular musical style in Vermont. Bluegrass features such musical instruments as the banjo, the mandolin, and the fiddle.

The arts are alive in Vermont. Live theater is performed throughout the state. There are a number of playhouses that stage high-energy performances from local and visiting theater troupes. The Vermont Stage Company tours all over the state, performing in venues, such as Burlington's Flynn Theater and the Barre Opera House. To experience a different kind of theater show, the Bread and Puppet Museum is the place to be. Housed in a 100-year-old barn in Glover, the Bread and Puppet Museum features one of the world's largest collections of giant puppets. These puppets are brightly-painted and crafted out of fabric and papier-mâché. In the summer, the Bread and Puppet Theater presents a variety of puppetry performances.

Every summer, the Bread and Puppet Theater presents a variety of outdoor performances. The performances feature live music, fresh-baked bread, and giant puppets.

The artist Norman Rockwell is best known for his depictions of American small-town life. He lived in the town of Arlington from 1939 to 1953, and many Arlington residents were featured in his work. Today, the Norman Rockwell Exhibition showcases many of his paintings. The exhibit is located in a nineteenth-century church, and several Arlington residents who modeled for his paintings serve as hosts.

Norman Rockwell painted 322 covers for *The Saturday Evening Post*. His first one appeared in 1916, when he was only 22 years of age.

SPORTS

The state's clean air and unspoiled beauty make outdoor recreation a popular pastime. In the warmer months, the Green Mountains welcome hikers and cyclists. The oldest long-distance hiking trail in the United States—the Long Trail—is a part of these mountains. The Long Trail traverses 270 miles from the Vermont–Massachusetts border in the south, all the way to the Canadian border in the north. The trail follows a challenging, rugged path through the mountains.

Other excellent hiking trails can be found in Vermont's state parks. The state's back roads offer many scenic routes for cyclists. Mountain biking is also popular on some Green Mountain National Forest trails.

There are more than 400 freshwater lakes and ponds in Vermont, providing residents and visitors with many locations for water sports. Sailing is enjoyed on Lake Champlain, while canoeing is popular on many of the mountain lakes. For experienced canoeists and kayakers, some stretches of the state's rivers offer great white-water challenges.

Vermont's Green Mountains are a hiker's paradise.

QUICK FACTS

Vermont's Long Trail served as the inspiration for the Appalachian Trail, a long-distance hiking trail that runs for about 2,160 miles from Maine to Georgia. The Appalachian Trail overlaps the Long Trail for about 100 miles in the southern part of Vermont.

Snowmobiling is a popular sport in Vermont. There are more than 3,600 miles of groomed snowmobiling trails throughout the state.

There are sixty-four golf courses in Vermont. One of the state's most challenging golf courses is at Stratton Mountain Country Club.

White-water rafting is a thrilling way to enjoy Vermont's rivers.

Skiing has long been the most popular sport in Vermont. In 1934, the very first ski tow in the United States began operation near Woodstock. Since then, more than twenty alpine ski resorts and about fifty cross-country ski centers have been established. Each winter, skiers from all over the country flock to Vermont to enjoy its excellent ski facilities. Downhill ski areas in the state vary from steep, challenging runs to family-oriented hills. Among the downhill resorts are Killington, Mount Snow, Smuggler's Notch, Stowe, Stratton, and Sugarbush. Cross-country ski trails are located throughout the state.

Many of the country's best skiers hail from Vermont. Exceptional alpine skiers, such as Betsy Snite, Andrea Meade, Suzy Chaffee, and Billy Kidd, all developed their talents on the Green Mountains. Bill Koch, a celebrated cross-country skier, is also from Vermont. In 1976, Koch became the first American to win an Olympic medal in a cross-country skiing event. Today, many Olympic hopefuls gather in Vermont to compete in one or more of the state's ski competitions.

With its numerous mountains and ski hills, snowboarding opportunities are abundant in Vermont.

QUICK FACTS

Vermont holds a number of important ski events and competitions throughout the year. Among the most popular are the NCAA Skiing Championships in Hancock and Ripton, the Annual Fred Harris Memorial Ski Jumping Tournament in Brattleboro, and the U.S. Open Snowboarding Championships in Stratton.

The "Snowseum," at the base of Mount Snow, is a museum dedicated to the history of skiing in the United States.

The Vermont Expos are a minor-league baseball team based in Burlington. The team's home ballpark is Centennial Field, located on the University of Vermont campus.

Brain Teasers

1

TRUE OR FALSE?

Vermont was the first New England state to build a railroad.

Answer: False. Vermont was the last of the New England states to build a railroad. Construction began in 1849.

2

TRUE OR FALSE?

Vermont is home to the oldest log cabin in the United States.

Answer: True. Hyde Log Cabin was built in Grand Isle in 1783.

3

MAKE A GUESS:

Who was the only president to be born on the fourth of July?

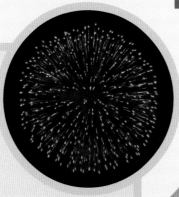

Answer: Calvin Coolidge. He was born in Plymouth Notch, Vermont, on July 4, 1872.

4

MULTIPLE CHOICE:

Which of the following was Vermonter Thomas Davenport responsible for inventing?

a. The electric railway

b. The electric motor

c. The electric printing press

d. All of the above

Answer: d. All of the above.

5

MAKE A GUESS:

What does Ben and Jerry's Ice Cream do with its ice-cream waste?

Answer: The company gives the waste to local farmers, who feed it to their pigs. It has been reported that most pigs like all of the flavors except Mint Oreo.

6

TRUE OR FALSE?

The first person to cross the entire United States by car was a doctor from Burlington.

Answer: True. The doctor made his journey in 1902.

7

TRUE OR FALSE?

Many Vermonters believe that there are sea monsters in Lake Champlain and Lake Memphremagog.

Answer: True. A monster nicknamed Champ is believed to live in Lake Champlain, and one called Memphre is believed to live in Lake Memphremagog. Many people claim to have seen these monsters, which are reportedly serpent-like in appearance.

8

MULTIPLE CHOICE:

James Wilson, of Bradford, Vermont, was responsible for creating:

a. the first camera made in the United States

b. the first globe made in the United States

c. the first answering machine made in the United States

d. the first wristwatch made in the United States

Answer: b. In 1810, James Wilson completed the first globe to be made in the country.

FOR MORE INFORMATION

Books

Arnosky, Jim. *Nearer Nature*. New York: Lothrop, Lee, and Shepard Books, 1996.

Aylesworth, Thomas, and Virginia Aylesworth. *Let's Discover the States: Northern New England.* New York: Chelsea House Publishers, 1998.

Dugger, Elizabeth L. *Adventure Guide to Vermont.* Massachusetts: Hunter Publishing Inc., 2000.

Web Sites

You can also go online and have a look at the following Web sites:

Vermont Information
http://www.vtliving.com

Vermont Tourism
http://www.1-800-vermont.com

History of the Trapp Family
http://www.trappfamily.com/history.html

Some Web sites stay current longer than others. To find other Vermont Web sites, enter search terms such as "Montpelier," "Green Mountains," "Trapp Family," or any other topic you want to research.

GLOSSARY

archeologists: scientists who study early peoples through artifacts and remains

balladeers: singers of folk songs

conifers: evergreen trees with needles and cones that keep their needles all winter

deciduous: trees and shrubs that shed leaves every year

haggis: a traditional Scottish pudding made of sheep or calf meat, which is boiled in the animal's stomach lining

jurisdiction: legal control over a region

mandatory: made into law, compulsory

migratory: seasonal movement of animals in search of food and shelter

negotiated: discussed, dealt, or bargained with another or others

nitrogen: a gaseous element that comprises about four-fifths of the atmosphere and is also found in animals and vegetables

powwow: a Native-American ceremony

quarries: large pits from which stone is extracted

semiconductors: basic electronic components used in computers and communications equipment

textile: relating to cloth or other fabric

trusses: frames designed to support bridges

INDEX